FOLLOW

YOUR

DREAMS

Scholastic Children's Books
Euston House,
24 Eversholt Street,

London NW1 1DB, UK

A division of Scholastic Ltd
London ~ New York ~ Toronto ~ Sydney ~ Auckland
Mexico City ~ New Delhi ~ Hong Kong

Published in the UK by Scholastic Ltd, 2018

Written by Emma Young

ISBN 978 1407 18902 4

Printed and bound by Bell & Bain Ltd, UK

2 4 6 8 10 9 7 5 3 1

www.scholastic.co.uk

Picture credits:

Front cover (left, centre, right) Mireya Acierto/Getty*; Craig Barritt/Getty*; Jon Kopaloff/Getty*

p7: (left to right) Jenny Anderson/Getty*; Tibrina Hobson/Getty*; Jeff Kravitz/Getty*; p10 (top left) Rodin Eckenroth/Getty*; (top right) Kevin Mazur/Fox/Getty*; (bottom left to right) Todd Williamson/Getty*; Jon Kopaloff/Getty*; Taylor Hill/Getty*; p11 (top) Paul Archuleta/Getty*; (bottom) Gabriel Olsen/Getty*; p12 (left to right) Kevin Mazur/Getty*; Jerod Harris/Getty*; p13 (top: left to right) Paul Redmond/Getty*; Frazer Harrison/AMA2015/Getty*; (bottom) Nicholas Hunt; Getty*; p.15 (left to right) Bruce Glikas/Getty*; Paul Archuleta/Getty*; Donato Sardella/Getty*; p18 (top) Frazer Harrison/Getty*; (bottom) Michael Bezjian; Getty*; p.19 (left) J. Merritt/Getty*; (right) Paul Archuleta/Getty*; p20 Taylor Hill/Getty*; p21 David Livingston/Getty*; p22 Pascal Le Segretain/Getty*; p23 Steve Jennings/Getty*; (bottom) Jean Baptiste Lacroix/Getty*; p24 NBC/Getty*; p25 Raymond Hall/Getty*; p26 Earl Gibson III/Getty*; p28 (left) Gregg DeGuire/Getty*; (right) Hollywood To You/Star Max/Getty*; p29 (top) David Livingston/Getty*; (bottom) Greg Doherty/Getty*; p30 (top) Kathy Hutchins/Shutterstock; (bottom left) Donna Svennevik /Getty*; (bottom right) Frazer Harrison/AMA2015/Getty*; p31 (left to right) Gregg DeGuire/Getty*; Axelle/Bauer-Griffin/Getty*; Axelle/Bauer-Griffin/Getty*; Paul Redmond/Getty*; p33 Jon Kopaloff/Getty*; p35 (left to right) Mireya Acierto/Getty*; Kathy Hutchins/Shutterstock Jon Kopaloff/Getty*; p36 (top left to right) Jeff Kravitz/Getty*; Jeff Kravitz/Getty*; Charley Gallay/Getty*; (bottom left to right) Steve Granitz/Getty*; Noam Galai/Getty*; Jim Spellman/Getty*; p37 (top) Tibrina Hobson/Getty*; (bottom) Frazer Harrison/Getty*; p38 Jo Hale/Getty*; p39 (top) David M. Benett/Getty* (bottom) Tinseltown/Shutterstock; p40 (top left) Alison Buck/Getty*; (top right) Jeffrey Mayer/Getty*; (middle left) Jeffrey Mayer/Getty* (middle right) David M. Benett/Getty*; (bottom left) David M. Benett/Getty*; (bottom right) MTV/TRL/Getty*; p45 Ori Gonian/Shutterstock; p46 (left) Matthias Nareyek/Getty*; (right) Tristar Media; p47 (top) Tristar Media/Getty*; (bottom) Tristar Media/Getty*; p48 (top and bottom) Kathy Hutchins/Shutterstock; p49 (top) Johnny Nunez/Getty*; (bottom) Amanda Edwards/Getty*; p50 Handout/Getty*; p51 (top) Raymond Hall/Getty*; (bottom) Joe Scarnici/Getty*; p52 (top) Kathy Hutchins/Shutterstock; (bottom) Frazer Harrison/Getty*; p53 (top to bottom) Alison Buck/Getty*; Jon Kopaloff/Getty*; MTV/TRL/Getty*; p54 Tristar Media/Getty*; p56 (left) Frazer Harrison/AMA2015/Getty*; (right) Image Group LA/Getty*; p57 (top) Jeff Kravitz/Getty*; (bottom) Ben Gabbe/Getty*; p58 Araya Diaz/Getty*; p59 Rodin Eckenroth/Getty*; p62 (top to bottom) gotpap/Star Max/Getty*; Gregg DeGuire/Getty*; Mireya Acierto/Getty*; Jeff Kravitz/Getty*; Steve Granitz/Getty*; p64 (top) Tinseltown/Shutterstock; (bottom) Jenny Anderson/Getty*; p65 (top) Tibrina Hobson/Getty* (bottom) Jeff Kravitz/Getty*; p66 (top) Tommaso Boddi; (bottom) Ga Fullner/Shutterstock; p67 (top) Dimitrios Kambouris/Getty*; (bottom) Mike Marsland/Getty*; p68 (top) Disney Channel/Getty*; (bottom) Pascal Le Segretain/Getty*; p69 (top) Mike Marsland/Getty*; (bottom) Todd Williamson/Getty*; p74 (top) Kevin Winter/Getty*; (bottom left to right) DFree/Shutterstock; Frederick M. Brown/Getty*; Alberto E. Rodriguez/Getty*; p75 (top) Tinseltown/Shutterstock; (bottom) CarlaVanWagoner/Shutterstock; p76 (top left to right) Bruce Glikas/Getty*; Tristar Media/Getty*; Kathy Hutchins/Shutterstock; (middle left to right) Tinseltown/Shutterstock; J. Victor Decolongon/Getty; MTV/TRL/Getty*; (bottom left to right) Noel Vasquez/Getty*; Ben Gabbe/Getty*; gotpap/Star Max/Getty*; p78 Steve Granitz/Getty*; p82, 83 gotpap/Star Max/Getty*; p84 (top left) Jaguar PS/Shutterstock; (bottom right) Jim Bennett/Getty* P85 (top left) DFree/Getty*; (middle right) Jamie Lamor Thompson/Shutterstock; (bottom left) Ga Fullner/Shutterstock p.87 (left to right) J. Victor Decolongon/Getty; Jeff Kravitz/Getty*; MTV/TRL/Getty*; p89 (left to right) Mireya Acierto/Getty*; Kathy Hutchins/Shutterstock; Jon Kopaloff/Getty*; p94 (left) Ga Fullner/Shutterstock; (right) gotpap/Star Max/Getty*; p95 (top left to right) J. Victor Decolongon/Getty; Jeff Kravitz/Getty*; MTV/TRL/Getty*

*Getty Images Entertainment

All illustrations courtesy of Shutterstock
Every effort has been made to ensure that this information is correct at the time of going to print. Any errors will be corrected upon reprint.

FOLLOW YOUR DREAMS

Written by Emma Young

SCHOLASTIC

WHAT'S INSIDE?

#BFF

HEY THERE!

Welcome to this celebration of talent, friendship and girl power, featuring your fave girls around the globe – from Maddie Ziegler to Lisa and Lena Mantler, Nia Sioux to JoJo Siwa – plus loads of others who have followed their dreams to get to the top!

As well as discovering tons of facts about these inspirational influencers, there are pages for you to record information about your own dreams and amazing squad. Plus create cute crafts, complete awesome quizzes and have fun getting to know your celeb besties.

This book can be read in any order so you can start at the beginning and work your way through, or just dive in on any page that catches your eye.

BE SMART AND STAY SAFE

Instagram, Musical.ly, YouTube and other platforms can be heaps of fun and a great way to stay in touch with your pals and fave celebs – but always make sure to stay safe online. Never give away your full name, address, phone number or details of your school. Don't post photos that might give away the location of your home or school (such as pics of your garden or your school uniform). If somebody is leaving comments that make you uncomfortable, talk to an adult.

FOLLOWING YOUR DREAMS

Dreaming of a future in the spotlight? Whether you're an amazing dancer like Maddie, an incredible actress like Storm or a bubbly all-rounder like JoJo, talent will only take you so far. Hard work and dedication are what really got your fave celebs to the top. Here are some top tips for making it.

Do what you love

If something is going to be a career, you have to spend a lot of time doing it – so think carefully about what your ambition is and DON'T do something just because your fave celeb does it. It's great to be inspired but your talent needs to come from the heart, too!

Practice makes perfect

If you want to succeed, you have to be prepared to work hard at your talent – and practise regularly, even if this sometimes means missing out on a cinema trip with your besties. Nia Sioux said that having to learn dance routines quickly was great training for her future career. 'Picking up choreography fast, it's one of the biggest things I am so thankful [to *Dance Moms*] for because doing that so many times every single week really made me a strong dancer.'

However, it's equally important not to work too hard – fun with your friends is healthy so make sure you leave SOME time for those cinema trips!

Get comfortable in front of a crowd

Maddie Ziegler says, 'Going on stage in front of a thousand people – that's kind of where I get my confidence from.' If a crowd that big sounds terrifying to you, try performing in front of a smaller group of people, maybe just your parents and your BFF, then slowly work your way up to a bigger audience.

Banish the nerves

Even the biggest stars can suffer from stage fright – it's natural, and just a reminder that whatever you are about to do means a lot to you. So whether you are preparing for a school talent show or your first ever audition, remember to take some deep breaths beforehand and remind yourself that even Storm Reid felt like this once. Ask yourself, what's the worst that can happen? Even if things go wrong this time, there will be other opportunities in the future – so you may as well go for it!

Keep smiling

The world of singing, dancing and acting can be tough – with all those auditions comes lots of rejection. And if you're posting content online, it can be easy to get caught up in negative comments. But if you stay positive and give out confident vibes, good things will come your way. Give it a hundred per cent and always channel your inner JoJo – work hard, believe in yourself and have fun!

Listen to feedback

It's important to get feedback so that you can continue to strengthen your skill. Whether it's your drama teacher, a singing coach or even your mum, ask someone to give you notes on what you are doing well and what you could be doing better. Even though it can be hard to hear that you're not doing things perfectly – yet! – every star needs feedback, so that they can work out how to keep getting better.

GETTING TO KNOW...
MADDIE ZIEGLER
MAGIC MADDIE'S GOT THE MOVES!

Busy Maddie's written two books for teens - an autobiography called *The Maddie Diaries: My Story* all about her rise to fame, and a novel about a talented dancer called *The Audition*.

Maddie hearts her BFF Millie Bobby Brown. She says, 'I connected with her the first time we met. I knew we were going to be friends.' Maddie keeps videos on her phone of Millie copying her dance routines from Dance Moms - cute!

On top of her other talents, Maddie has her own clothing range called Maddie Style. She says, 'The design process is my favourite part. I pull a lot of ideas from Instagram, my own closet (wardrobe) and friends. We then design, test everything, and I put my own spin on them.'

#BFF

Maddie rocks loads of different hairstyles - which is your fave?

Maddie has always loved to dance! She started ballet lessons when she was just two years old, and it's been a passion ever since. She took part in six seasons of the US TV programme *Dance Moms* – giving audiences around the world a glimpse into the hard work and determination needed to succeed in the competitive world of dance. This talented teen was scouted by singer Sia and has appeared in several of her music videos. From her debut role in *The Book of Henry*, to voicing the villain in the animated film *Ballerina*, multi-talented Maddie is also an awesome actor.

Name: Madison Nicole Ziegler

Date of birth: 30 September 2002

Famous for: Starring in *Dance Moms*

Favourite colour: Purple

Famous sister: Mackenzie Ziegler

Famous BFF: Millie Bobby Brown

Random fact: Maddie was originally named Taylor, but her parents changed her name to Madison when she was two days old!

INTERNET

CELEBRITY BESTIES

Busy schedules, around-the-world tours and regular rehearsals can be super tiring, so it's important to have good pals to turn to. Everyone needs a best friend – to share the good times with and for when the going gets tough. Say hi to some of the cutest girl crews around.

MADDIE & MILLIE

Maddie says, 'Millie likes to dress up and impersonate all of my dances ... it's really, really funny!'

DOVE & SOFIA

Dove and Sofia have a real-life friendship just like their characters Mal and Evie in the *Descendants* films. Their fans call them Dofia!

JOJO & NIA

JoJo and Nia have been dancing together since they were little!

SOPHIA GRACE & ROSIE

Taking on the world is easy with your cousin by your side!

ZENDAYA & YARA

Talented pals Zendaya and Yara are both amazing actors.

WHO'S YOUR CELEB BFF?

Answer the questions to find your perfect celebrity match.

1 I like people who are:

a) bubbly ☐

b) organized ☐

c) creative ☐

2 My fave activities to do with my friends are:

a) playing pranks and making slime ☐

b) trying on outfits and doing makeovers ☐

c) making up songs and dance routines ☐

3 If me and my friend were spending the weekend together we would:

a) do something crazy and random ☐

b) have a cosy night in, drink hot chocolate and paint each other's nails ☐

c) invite some pals round and have a dance-off ☐

4 I love my BFF because she:

a) makes me spit out my drink laughing ☐

b) is a really good listener ☐

c) is always the life and soul of the party ☐

5 My BFF's fave celeb is:

a) Miranda Sings ☐

b) Millie Bobby Brown ☐

c) Zendaya ☐

6

My squad is made up of:

a) anyone who's up for some games and LOLZ – including my pets! ☐

b) one or two very close pals ☐

c) loads of friends with different interests ☐

Now find out who your celeb BFF is:

Mostly As: Your celeb BFF is ... JoJo Siwa! Bubbly and fun-loving, this bow-obsessed girl is a laugh a minute and has the most infectious giggle on the planet!

Mostly Bs: Your celeb BFF is ... Maddie Ziegler! She loves having sleepovers and giving her pals cute makeovers. She's always there to give a listening ear.

Mostly Cs: Your celeb BFF is ... Storm Reid! Outgoing and creative, she loves to surround herself with people. Her positive attitude to life makes her a fab friend to have.

Now you know who your celeb BFF is, fill in this section about your best friend IRL.

My BFF's name:

....

My BFF's nickname:

....

Where we met:

....

Stick a photo of you and your BFF here.

#BFF

SLEEPOVER GOALS

Sleepovers provide the perfect opportunity to get your friends together to collab on a vlog, record a Musical.ly vid, chat about your favourite online influencers, eat ALL the snacks and get absolutely zero winks. Plan your perfect sleepover here.

Who's on the guest list?

Millie Bobby Brown's first ever sleepover was with Maddie Ziegler – and it was a TOTAL disaster. At three o'clock in the morning, the fire alarm went off and the girls had to evacuate the building!

#BFF

Time to stock up on snacks. What's on the menu?

Pizza ☐
Crunchy veg and dips ☐
Smoothies ☐

Cupcakes ☐
Popcorn ☐
Sweets ☐

Other ideas:
....
....
....

Let's get comfy ... what's the dress code?

Cute PJs

Animal onesies

T-shirt nighties

(... and don't forget the fluffy slippers!)

What are you going to get up to?

Making slime

Trying new hairstyles

Doing DIY mermaid manicures

Chatting the night away

Making Musical.ly vids

Watching films

Other ideas:

....

....

....

....

For girl band Little Mix, sleepovers give them a chance to hang out away from the cameras, come up with new lyrics, practise their music and share secrets. Can we have an invite to the next one, please?

Turn back to page 7 for tips about staying safe online and remember to check with a parent or guardian before posting content.

GETTING TO KNOW... LAUREN ORLANDO

LOVELY LAUREN IS AN ALL-ROUND SUPERSTAR!

Lauren and her older brother Johnny attend a school for teens who work in showbiz.

Lauren loves anything creative – acting, drawing, singing, photography or dancing. She also enjoys sports, especially ice hockey.

My most-watched Lauren Orlando video is:

Eat It or Wear It Challenge (Orlandos vs Zieglers)

Try Not to Laugh Challenge (with Mackenzie Ziegler)

Smoothie Challenge (with Johnny Orlando)

Lauren was only seven when she started appearing in her brother Johnny's YouTube videos – and she hasn't looked back since. She started her own channel in 2013, uploading loads of fun challenges, DIYs and vlogs. Lauren and Johnny are pals with the Ziegler sisters and sometimes film hilarious challenges together.

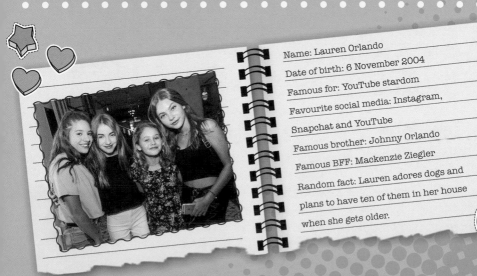

Name: Lauren Orlando

Date of birth: 6 November 2004

Famous for: YouTube stardom

Favourite social media: Instagram, Snapchat and YouTube

Famous brother: Johnny Orlando

Famous BFF: Mackenzie Ziegler

Random fact: Lauren adores dogs and plans to have ten of them in her house when she gets older.

GIRL GANG

INTERNET

HIDDEN TALENTS

Despite their packed schedules, today's influencers know that it's important to make time to do something you love ... other than your main talent! Whether they're inclined to pick up a paintbrush or a wooden spoon – some of these celebs' secret skills may surprise you.

Celeb: Maddie Ziegler
Hobby: hair and make-up

Maddie has always been passionate about all things beauty and says, 'If I weren't a dancer, I'd be a hair and make-up artist.' She loves featuring hair tutorials on her YouTube channel, using her sister as a model. Luckily her talent has grown over the years: when Maddie was five, she accidentally burned Mackenzie's face while curling her hair for a party. Ouch!

Celeb: Chloe Lukasiak
Hobby: reading

Chloe is a self-confessed nerd and always had her nose stuck in a book growing up – when she wasn't dancing, of course. And now she's launched her own book club! Chloe tells her fans, 'Reading has always been extremely important to me and I've always wanted to find a way to share my love for books with you.' You can find lots of ways to join in with Chloe's book club online.

Celeb: Emma Watson
Hobby: painting

When she's not busy starring in her latest blockbuster, *Beauty and the Beast* star Emma Watson can often be found wielding a paintbrush! She especially enjoys painting people's expressions and faces – the walls of her house are decorated with her paintings. While Emma keeps her hobby quite private, she admits it's very important to her, saying, 'I love it and have a need to do it.'

Celeb: Taylor Swift
Hobby: baking

Before T-Swift was a world famous icon, she loved to cook – and she still enjoys baking cookies and cakes in her downtime. She proudly posts the results of her bakes on Instagram, and these have included a delicious-looking apple pie, M&M chocolate chip cookies and an American flag cake. Is there ANYTHING this girl can't do? YouTuber Zoella is also a huge baking fan and even starred on the *Great Comic Relief Bake-Off*.

Celeb: Millie Bobby Brown
Hobby: boxing

From Thai boxing to Jiu-Jitsu, Millie loves to put on her gloves and work out. Just like her tough *Stranger Things* character, Eleven, she's not one to shy away from a fight and even has a punch bag in her back garden!

FLUFFY AND FAMOUS

BFFs come in all shapes and sizes – and species. Say hi to some famous pets ... the good, the bad and the fluffy!

Sophia Grace prefers cats to dogs because they're more chilled. She has a tabby cat named Poppy.

She's got me working like a dog!

Ariana Grande adopted her gorgeous dog, Toulouse, from an animal shelter.

At the end of a tour, Taylor Swift loves coming home to her cats, Olivia and Meredith.

If a flea lands on me, I just *Shake It Off!*

Zoella loves her pup Nala and even threw her a first birthday party with balloons and delicious home-made 'pupcakes'!

Mackenzie Ziegler's super-cute pup, Maliboo, is a cross between a poodle and a Maltese! Mackenzie was given Maliboo by her dance teacher. The adorable dog often features on the Ziegler girls' Instagram accounts.

CUTE

PAMPERED PETS

Cute outfits and sparkly accessories – it's not just celebrity humans that can dress to impress.

Twinning is winning!

JoJo's pup BowBow is a teeny tiny teacup Yorkie, and weighed only 500 grams when JoJo got her. This pampered pup even has her own Instagram account and loves getting kisses from her owner!

CUTE

Design a new bow for BowBow!

Do you have a pet? Stick in a photo or draw a picture of them here. If you don't have your own pet, use this space to draw a picture of your dream fluffy friend.

Name:

• 27 •

GETTING TO KNOW...
NIA SIOUX

CONFIDENCE AND HARD WORK TOOK NIA TO THE TOP!

Nia has an older brother named Evan Frazier Jr and a little brother named William Frazier. She is close to her mum, Holly, who she says is her best friend.

Nia shares an inspirational person each week on #RoleModelMonday. One of her role models was the amazing Marley Dias, who launched #1000BlackGirlBooks, a campaign to collect and donate 1,000 books that feature black girls as the main character.

Nia's newest project, *Summer Dance*, is a movie about a young dancer who falls in love and finds herself having to balance her relationship and pursuing her dreams. Nia plays the main character, Jasmine.

Which dance move was Nia famous for on *Dance Moms*?
Flick to page 94 to see if you were right!

A Death drip

B Death drop

C Death dab

Nia has been dancing since she was tiny, and found fame alongside the other stars of *Dance Moms*. She finally left the show at the age of sixteen to pursue new avenues. She nabbed a role in the musical *Trip of Love*, and plans to follow her dream of a career on Broadway. Nia's motto is 'star in your own life' – she even wrote a song with this inspiring phrase as the title. The music video was a mega hit with nearly 12 million views on YouTube! Nia inspires her fans to think positive and says that 'having confidence changes everything.'

Name: Nia Sioux Frazier

Singer name: Nia Sioux

Date of birth: 20 June 2001

Famous for: appearing on *Dance Moms* for seven seasons running, now a singer and actor

Favourite dance styles: contemporary and musical theatre

Random fact: her favourite films are Pitch Perfect and Frozen

INTERNET

DANCE, DREAM, BELIEVE

What do JoJo, Maddie, Mackenzie, Nia and Chloe all have in common? They all sprang to fame on hit show *Dance Moms*! This amazing programme about the drama of dance competitions in the US began in 2011 and since then there have been hundreds of dance routines, oodles of nerves and a LOT of costume disasters – plus friendships, rivalries and mums getting competitive!

The dream team back in 2012

#BFF

The girls won countless competitions with their incredible routines

Dancers Kendall, JoJo and Nia at JoJo's 13th birthday party

Say what?

Seven seasons of *Dance Moms* gave us some pretty funny sound bites!

'Of course I wanna win, I'm Maddie.' Maddie Ziegler

'People call me energy in a bottle.' JoJo Siwa

'When Maddie would come over to my house we would go into my mom's office where her computer was and we would make up the craziest dances... We still do.'
Kendall Vertes

'I don't want to be on Broadway. I just want to stay at home and eat chips.' Mackenzie Ziegler

Who's your fave mum and daughter combo?

1. Holly and Nia

2. Jill and Kendall

3. Christi and Chloe

4. Jesslyn and JoJo

MAKE YOUR MOVE

From pirouettes to pliés, jetés to arabesques the *Dance Moms* girls nailed the techniques of heaps of different dance styles. Get clued up on their favourite moves.

Cartwheel cool!

Mackenzie's awesome acrobatic skills got more impressive with every season. One of her favourite acro tricks was a rolling tinsica – a twisting cartwheel where the dancer ends up in the same position as she started.

Hands up!

A perfectly executed split handstand would have been impressive enough, but in her signature one-handed split, JoJo halved the number of hands and doubled the stakes!

Death drop!

Nia learned her signature move in series one, and still loves performing it. This dramatic fall and pose forms the perfect ending to several of her solos.

Take a leap!

Known for her perfect technique, Maddie's 'switch sissone' took audiences' breath away. In this beautiful leap, the dancer jumps from two feet, then splits their legs like scissors.

What's your favourite dance style?

Jazz

Musical theatre

Lyrical

Contemporary

Ballet

Acrobatic

When the music starts you can find me...

In the middle of the dance floor

Bopping in a circle with my friends

On the sidelines tapping my feet

What's your signature dance move?

Awkward shuffling

Flossing

The dab

SQUAD SCRAPBOOK

As well as being a tight dancing team, the *Dance Moms* girls grew up as best friends and knew everything about each other. Want your squad to be as tight as theirs? Follow these instructions to make a book full of info about your besties, with your besties.

You will need

A blank notebook

Colourful pens

Cute stickers

Your favourite photos

Most importantly ... your BFFs!

Instructions

1
Take the notebook and decorate the cover. Do this together, taking it in turns to add everyone's doodles, drawings, stickers and photos.

2
Give the book a special title – you could name it after the initials of your squad, or combine all your nicknames, or come up with something completely new.

3 Make the first page of the notebook a sign-in page, where each friend writes their name and a symbol (like an emoji or animal) that represents them.

4 On top of each page, take turns writing a question, using your symbols to mark whose turn it is.

Questions could be silly:

If you could be any type of fish, what fish would you be?

Or serious:

Which band or musician would you most like to see perform live?

Or you could even ask your friends to share a secret:

What is your most embarrassing moment of last year?

Once you've written several questions, pass the book around again to scribble down your answers.

5 Keep the notebook in a safe place. Every time you and your friends get together, add more questions for everyone to answer. Soon you'll have an amazing book bursting with info about you and your crew which you can treasure always!

Remember, it's totally OK if one of the sisterhood doesn't want to share an answer. They can skip their go or just draw their symbol to still take part. No pressure!

GETTING TO KNOW...
JOJO SIWA
BUBBLY JOJO IS BURSTING WITH ENERGY!

BEFORE

Did you know you that there is a JoJo Siwa Halloween costume, complete with bow and glittery skirt? Yes please!

Good friends with her *Dance Moms* co-stars like Nia Sioux, JoJo also makes time for her BFFs in her home town and FaceTimes them as often as she can.

JoJo ends her funny vlogs by pouring fruit juice all over herself. She's even been slimed live on stage!

AFTER

JoJo's 'cute little snuggle muffin' BowBow the dog takes off JoJo's socks for her every night.

JoJo is never seen without one of her colourful signature bows! Pick your fave from the three below.

JoJo is one inspiring girl. She can dance, sing, perform AND she's started her own bow business, encouraging others around the world to wear a bright and beautiful bow as a symbol of 'power, confidence, believing-ness'. So much more than a hair bow, this business-minded fifteen-year-old's brand now spans everything from duvet covers to karaoke machines. And it's easy to see why she's doing so well – JoJo's positive song about ignoring bullies, "Boomerang" has been watched nearly half a BILLION times on YouTube.

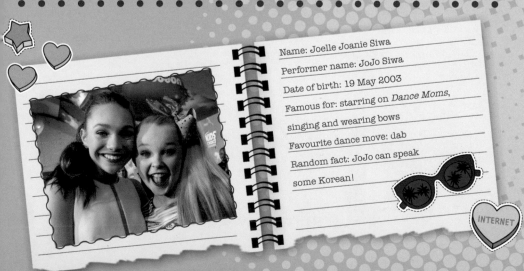

Name: Joelle Joanie Siwa

Performer name: JoJo Siwa

Date of birth: 19 May 2003

Famous for: starring on *Dance Moms*, singing and wearing bows

Favourite dance move: dab

Random fact: JoJo can speak some Korean!

VLOGGING PALS

Famous YouTubers like Zoella, Tanya and Noodlerella love to vlog, sharing videos all about their lives and interests with their fans. Sometimes, instead of vlogging alone, they like to buddy up and film with their besties for double the fun!

SevenSuperGirls post a new video every day. The girls take it in turns to film videos. They are the largest all-girl collaboration on YouTube with over 8 million subscribers!

Noodlerella – aka Connie Glynn – is part of an online group called G4laxygirls. They love all things pink, anime and Japan-related and often appear in each other's travel vlogs.

Zoella and Tanya Burr love hanging out together and filming at each other's houses. Their dogs Nala and Martha are friends and at Christmas the girls like to wear matching pyjamas.

#BFF

MEMORY

Sparkle

Miranda Sings and JoJo Siwa often make silly videos together, like slime fights and funny dance tutorials!

Mum-collabs are fun too! B2cutecupcakes does fun challenges with her mum and seven-year-old Darcy sometimes guest stars on her mum SprinkleOfGlitter's channel.

BE COOL

DREAM COLLAB

Megan Lytle

Lilly Singh

Veronica and Vanessa Merrell

Tanya Burr

Zoella and Louise Pentland

Miranda Sings
(aka Colleen Ballinger)

Imagine if you could set up a channel with your fave YouTuber. Use this page to dream it up.

Which YouTuber?
....

What would your channel name be?
(For example, SevenSuperGirls, DanandPhilGames)
....

oh yeah

How often would you vlog?
....

#BFF

What would your videos be about? Tick as many as you want, or come up with your own ideas!

				Other ideas:
Baking	☐	Unboxings	☐	....
Gaming	☐	Dance routines	☐	....
Beauty	☐	Books	☐	....
Pranks	☐			

'The joy of YouTube is that you can create content about anything you feel passionate about, however silly.' Zoella

LIVE IT, FILM IT

The magic of vlogging is that anyone can do it. All you need is an idea, a camera and an Internet connection. It's important to work on your presenting skills – if you dream of becoming a top vlogger then practise chatting to a camera to get comfortable before you share footage online.

For your first few vlogs try writing a rough script or outline, so you don't get stuck for what to say! Use these pages to scribble down your ideas.

Turn back to page 7 for tips about staying safe online and remember to check with a parent or guardian before posting content.

#BFF

A bedroom tour, shopping haul or funny challenge – check out vlogs from top YouTubers to get ideas.

SLIME TIME

JoJo Siwa, Sophia Grace, Annie LeBlanc – all your fave influencers have a big obsession. It's satisfying, stretchy and very, very ... slimey! Make your own JoJo-inspired glitter slime in six simple steps. Ask an adult to help you find the ingredients.

You will need:

- PVA or clear glue
- Bicarbonate of soda
- Skewer
- Gel food colouring (optional)
- Contact lens solution (ask a parent to make sure the one you buy contains boric acid)
- Glitter or sequins

Time to make slime!

① Tip 150 millilitres of PVA glue into a clean bowl.

② Add 1 teaspoon of bicarbonate of soda and mix them together.

③ If you want to add colouring this is the best time to do it. Dip a skewer into the gel food colouring to pick up a blob, then stir it into the mixture until the colour has spread.

4 Next add 1 tablespoon of contact lens solution. Mix with a spoon until the mixture starts to become stringy, coming away from the edges of the bowl.

5 Take it out of the bowl and knead it between your hands. It will start off sticking to them but within about 20 seconds it will firm up and stick only to itself, becoming elastic and super stretchy. (If it's still too sticky then add a few more drops of contact lens solution until it's just right.)

6 Finally, add the glitter and/ or sequins to the mixture. Woohoo – your slime is ready! Stretch it, squish it or snip it with scissors!

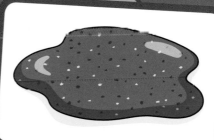

Stretch it!

Squish it!

Some people have allergies to slime ingredients – check with a parent before you begin and never make slime without adult supervision.

GETTING TO KNOW...
LISA AND LENA MANTLER
DOUBLE THE TROUBLE AND DOUBLE THE TALENT!

The trendy twins both love fashion! Lisa loves to buy her clothes from the high street, while Lena prefers to order them online. They also have their own clothing line and enjoy hanging out at fashion shows.

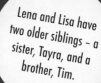

Lena and Lisa have two older siblings – a sister, Tayra, and a brother, Tim.

Lisa and Lena have over 21 million followers on Musical.ly, despite the fact they only spend about twenty minutes a day working on their viral videos.

What are your fave tunes to lip sync to?

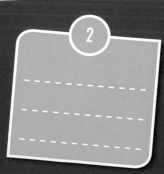

1 ❤️
- - - - - - - - -
- - - - - - - - -
- - - - - - - - -

2
- - - - - - - - -
- - - - - - - - -
- - - - - - - - -

3
- - - - - - - - -
- - - - - - - - -
- - - - - - - - -

Identical twins Lena and Lisa shot to fame after showcasing their amazing lip sync videos on app Musical.ly. Their adorable synchronized dances and complementary outfits have made them a huge hit both at home in Germany, and all around the world. Even their biggest fans sometimes find it hard to tell the musers apart! Hint: Lena is a bit taller than Lisa and Lisa has a birthmark on her nose.

Names: Lisa and Lena Mantler

Nickname: Leli

Date of birth: 17 June 2002

Famous for: Lip-syncing videos

Favourite social media: Musical.ly, Instagram

Favourite accessory: Hats and caps

Random fact: Lena is the slightly older twin.

INTERNET

SISTER, SISTER

Just like Lena and Lisa, these sisters love working together – and having fun, of course!

Maddie and Mackenzie Ziegler regularly pop up in each other's social media posts. Though Maddie was less than impressed when she spotted Kenzie wearing her jeans on Instagram and told her off in the comments. Whoops... The Ziegler sisters also love taking part in sibling challenges with Lauren and Johnny Orlando.

Identical twins Brooklyn and Bailey McKnight have a popular fashion and beauty channel, BrooklynAndBailey. They first appeared on YouTube at eighteen months old as models on Cute Girls Hairstyles, the channel set up by their mum.

YouTube stars Gracie, Olivia, Sierra and Madison – aka the Haschak Sisters – love music, gymnastics competitions and doggy fashion shows!

#BFF

The Merrell twins, Vanessa and Veronica, post funny sketches and music covers on their joint YouTube channel.

FABULOUS FASHION

Stuck for what to wear? Here's some style inspo from some of the coolest gals around.

'Do what makes you comfortable and that's how you'll look your best!' Ariana Grande

JoJo Siwa owns over a thousand bows – perfect for jazzing up any outfit!

Maddie Ziegler says, 'Zendaya is a really big inspiration for me in the fashion world!'

BE COOL

Chloe Lukasiak isn't afraid of bold colours and clashing prints – and she always looks awesome!

Sparkle

'I'm a girl that loves life, I love doing what I do and I'm obsessed with fashion.'
Storm Reid

Sophia Grace usually keeps it casual with jeans and a T-shirt, but glams up with a pretty frock and bag for an awards do. Her favourite shops are Topshop, New Look and River Island.

FASHION MATCH

Draw a line to match the celeb to the accessory they sometimes wear when performing.

Answers on page 94

OUTFIT GOALS

Lisa and Lena are seriously stylish twins – use this page to design a new outfit for their wardrobe!

Describe your perfect wardrobe:

....

....

....

....

My fave colours to wear are:

I am happiest in:

Leggings and a T-shirt ☐

A pretty dress ☐

A tracksuit and trainers ☐

A cute skirt and top ☐

Other ideas

....

....

....

List three people whose style you admire. (You can flick through this book for ideas!)

1. ....

2. ....

3. ....

Where do you like to buy your clothes?

1. ....

2. ....

3. ....

4. ....

GETTING TO KNOW...
SOPHIA GRACE BROWNLEE
MOVE OVER TUTUS AND TIARAS, SOPHIA'S ALL GROWN UP

Friendship is really important to Sophia Grace and she loves talking to her BFFs. She says: 'They can always cheer me up because they're really funny and that's why I'm friends with them!' Bonus fact: she also listens to happy music and eats ice cream when she's feeling down.

Now she writes her own top tunes, like "Best Friends", "Why U Mad?" and "Girl in the Mirror". She gets her ideas from her real-life friendships.

Sophia Grace and Rosie have performed on TV numerous times and have even shot their own movie, *Sophia Grace and Rosie's Royal Adventure*. There are rumours of a sequel...

What's your fave Sophia Grace lyric?

'Hey, well, excuse me if I think that I'm pretty' (from "Girl in the Mirror")

'Loving yourself should always come first' (from "Why U Mad?")

'I'm your number one girl, I'm your best friend' (from "Best Friends")

Sophia Grace is from Essex in England. When she was just eight years old, Sophia skyrocketed to fame with her younger cousin Rosie, when their cover of Nicki Minaj's song "Super Bass" went viral. The adorable duo then went on to have a regular spot on a US chat show, interviewing celebs including Miley Cyrus, Taylor Swift and Justin Bieber. Now all grown up, Sophia's following in the footsteps of her idols and launching a music career.

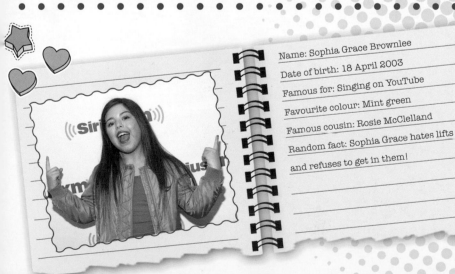

Name: Sophia Grace Brownlee

Date of birth: 18 April 2003

Famous for: Singing on YouTube

Favourite colour: Mint green

Famous cousin: Rosie McClelland

Random fact: Sophia Grace hates lifts and refuses to get in them!

INTERNET

TOP TEES

What better way to make a statement than with your T-shirt?
Use these pages to design your dream slogan tee.

Choose a slogan for your T-shirt:

Messy hair don't care ☐

100% chill ☐

Weekend vibes ☐

I ❤ my BFF ☐

Or write your own slogan here:

....

....

Choose a background colour for your T-shirt:

White ☐

Black ☐

Grey ☐

Green ☐

Choose a colour for the slogan:

Rainbow glitter ☐

Silver ☐

Black ☐

Pink ☐

Draw your T-shirt here:

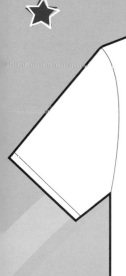

MUSE ON

Love lip syncing with your bestie? If so, Musical.ly is the app for you! It's a creative space where users can perform, share, discover and be discovered in 15-second video clips. Use this page to fill in your Musical.ly info.

A muser's only limits are time (15 seconds), age (you must be aged 13 or over) and imagination.

My top three musers:

1. ....

2. ....

3. ....

Things that make these musers stand out:

1. ....

2. ....

3. ....

My top three Musical.ly songs:

1. ....
2. ....
3. ....

Muser I'd most like to duet with:

....

Musical.ly category I watch the most:

....

I would send hearts to:

....

Would you rather:

Hit one million Musical.ly followers OR get 2 million hearts?

....

Meet Lisa and Lena Mantler OR Max and Harvey Mills?

....

Post a Musical.ly with a bogey up your nose OR lipstick on your teeth?

....

Create a duet with Sophia Grace OR Maddie Ziegler?

....

MAKING MUSIC

Move over Taylor Swift, Beyoncé and Adele, there's some new talent in town! But can you match the lyric with the artist? Draw a line to the photo of the right talented girl, then check your answers on page 94.

A
Don't hate on the happy, it's never gonna work,
Loving yourself should always come first.

1
Mackenzie Ziegler,
"Breathe"

B
Everybody has a dream that they need to follow,
All you got to do is believe.

2
Kendall K,
"Wear 'Em Out"

C
They can keep talking their talk,
But I'm a keep walking my walk
And I won't hear a sound.

3
Nia Sioux,
"Star in Your Own Life"

D
Feel the sunlight on your skin,
Keep your heartbeat beatin',
Go on, go on, breathe in.

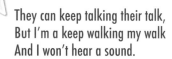

4
Sophia Grace,
"Why U Mad?"

E
Step on the stage,
Give a round of applause,
'Cause you know I run this place.

5
JoJo Siwa,
"Boomerang"

Stuck for ideas? Start off by writing a new verse for one of your fave songs, then develop it into something original.

WISE WORDS

Take some life advice from the girls who are nailing it.

"

Selena Gomez on friendship:

'If you have three people in your life that you can trust, you can consider yourself the luckiest person in the whole world.'

"

Sophia Grace on bullying:

'Be kind to the kid being bullied. Show them that you care by trying to include them. Sit with them at lunch or on the bus, talk to them at school or invite them to do something.'

JoJo Siwa on being yourself:

'I just wanna be a kid and I just wanna have fun. I just wanna do what I do and I think people really like that about me.'

Storm Reid on achieving your dreams:

'You can be a superhero and you rock and you can conquer the world and you are beautiful just the way you are.'

GETTING TO KNOW... STORM REID

AN ACTRESS WHO'S TAKING THE WORLD BY STORM

Storm used to worry that she was too tall for her age but Oprah Winfrey told her, 'Don't waste energy on things you can't change.'

Storm had a fab time acting with Rowan Blanchard in *A Wrinkle in Time*. The fashion-loving girls are good pals on and off screen.

Storm loves asking her mum for advice. She says her mum 'doesn't care if I stop acting tomorrow, she just wants the best for me.' Aww!

#BFF

There are three sneaky differences between these two pics of Storm. Place a circle around each one.

Storm has been destined for fame from a young ago! She starred in her first advert when she was three and a short film when she was nine. Now the star of *A Wrinkle in Time* alongside superstars Oprah Winfrey, Reese Witherspoon and Mindy Kaling, Storm wants to inspire other girls around the world to believe in themselves and follow their dreams.

Name: Storm Reid

Date of birth: 1 July 2003

Famous for: starring in *A Wrinkle in Time*

Favourite snack: mint oreos

Random fact: her fave book as a kid was *Where the Wild Things Are*.

MOVIE MAGIC

Go behind the scenes and discover some fun facts about your fave actors.

Dove Cameron wore six different wigs in *Descendants 2* and her costumes were made of leather, which meant she was often boiling hot on set!

Before starring as Belle in *Beauty and the Beast*, Emma Watson watched the original animated film as a child. She says: 'I can't even think how many times I watched it ... I knew all the words by heart. I knew all the songs by heart.' Sounds like good research, Emma!

Storm Reid thought she'd messed up her first audition for *A Wrinkle In Time* and was surprised to get through to the next stage. She says, 'I had it set in my mind already that I wasn't gonna get it. And then, when I got called for a callback, I was like, "Oh, wow, okay!"'

Maddie Ziegler recorded all her lines for the animated film *Ballerina* (called *Leap!* in the US) in just one day. She said her time on *Dance Moms* helped her to understand her character, a snobby ballerina who wants to be a star. She said that she knows 'what it's like to want that spot and to become the best.'

FILM FAVES

My fave TV shows are:

1. ....

2. ....

3. ....

My fave films are:

1. ....

2. ....

3. ....

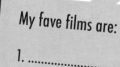

My fave actors are:

1. ....

2. ....

3. ....

My fave cinema snack is:

Sweet popcorn ☐

Salty popcorn ☐

Nachos ☐

Pick 'n' mix ☐

Chocolate ☐

Other: ☐

....

....

....

LIGHTS, CAMERA, ACTION

Ever dreamed about making or starring in your own film?
Here is your chance to put your ideas down on paper.

My film would be called:

....

It would be about:

....

....

....

....

....

....

....

It would star the following people:

....

....

....

....

You can choose anyone –
your BFF, your sister, your
fave celebs, even yourself...

You could be inspired by
your favourite book or
your own life!

COMING SOON TO A CINEMA NEAR YOU!

GETTING TO KNOW...
MILLIE BOBBY BROWN
MARVELLOUS MILLIE HAS SUPERPOWERS BOTH ON AND OFF SCREEN!

Millie is home-schooled and has to fit homework around her acting jobs. She says it can sometimes get a bit lonely not being at school. Luckily, she has lots of showbiz friends! Millie's girl squad includes BFF Maddie Ziegler and singer Grace Vanderwaal.

On Sundays Millie and her whole family like to go for a roast dinner before coming home and cosying up in front of a film.

Kind-hearted Millie helped out a fan when nobody turned up to his *Stranger Things*-themed birthday party. She tweeted, 'I think you're awesome and next year I would like an invite... Please?'

Millie loves to dress up for big events – vote for your fave outfit here!

Brit-born actress Millie's big break came when she scored the role of *Stranger Things* character, Eleven. This unlikely superhero helps save her town from the dark creatures of the Upside-Down. Millie bravely shaved her head for the role. She even uploaded a YouTube vid of her lovely locks being cut!

Name: Millie Bobby Brown

Date of birth: 19 February 2004

Famous for: starring in TV show

Stranger Things

Favourite outfit: onesie

Famous BFF: Maddie Ziegler

Random fact: she loves the Kardashians ...

Kourtney is her fave!

INTERNET

CAPTION QUEENS

Adorable compliments, cute emojis or snappy hashtags – these ladies know how to sum up a photo in a short phrase. See if you can come up with some celeb-worthy captions for these perfect pics.

New emojis are always being released, so why not make up one of your own? Draw it here and make a note of what it means!

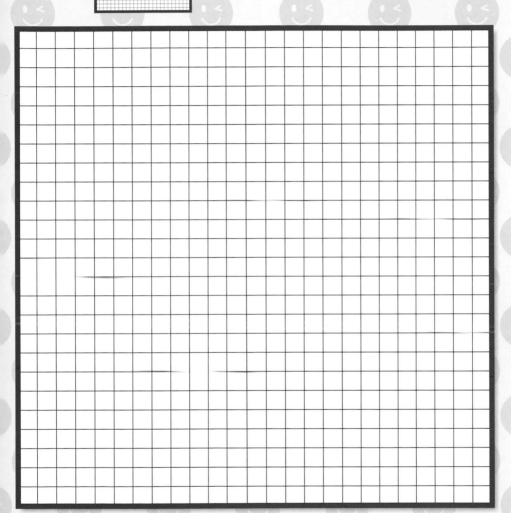

Name of emoji:

....

What it means:

....

ALL-STAR HOLIDAYS

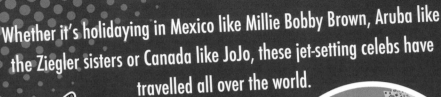

Whether it's holidaying in Mexico like Millie Bobby Brown, Aruba like the Ziegler sisters or Canada like JoJo, these jet-setting celebs have travelled all over the world.

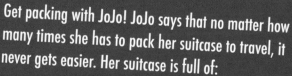

Get packing with JoJo! JoJo says that no matter how many times she has to pack her suitcase to travel, it never gets easier. Her suitcase is full of:

Glittery outfits

Converse trainers in lots of different colours

Unicorn hoodies

Make-up

Camera equipment

And – of course – bows!

Tip: use this page next time you are going on holiday!

What to pack in my suitcase:

....

....

....

....

....

DREAM TRIP

Name three places you've travelled to:

1. ....

2. ....

3. ....

Name three places you'd love to travel to:

1. ....

2. ....

3. ....

Which BFF would you take on a cruise?

....

Which BFF would you take to Disney World?

....

Which BFF would you take to the seaside?

....

Who would be your fave celeb travel companion?

....

SPOT THE LOT

There are five sneaky differences between these two pics of Mackenzie, Johnny and Lauren. Place a circle around each one.

Answers on page 94

GIRL POWER

With the world watching their every move, these amazing girls are uniquely positioned to use their platforms to effect change. Go girls!

Zendaya

As well as being an actress, singer, dancer and all-round fashionista, Zendaya still manages to leave time in her busy schedule to give back to the community. The list of charities Zendaya supports is endless – she even celebrated her eighteenth birthday raising money for the charity feedONE and continues to champion diversity, equality and body positivity!

Mikaila Ulmer

After being stung by a bee – not once but twice – Mikaila took it upon herself to find out about these insects. She learned that these buzzing little wonders not only play an important role in our ecosystem but also are sadly on their way to extinction. Inspired to make a change, she started her own lemonade stand and donated a portion of the profits to honeybee advocate groups. Fast forward a few years and she's the CEO of her very own company, Me & the Bees Lemonade.

Hailee Steinfeld

Having received an Oscar nomination at only fourteen years old, Hailee continues to take the film industry by storm. She makes a point of inspiring others through her music and films, encouraging people to stand up for what they believe in. In 2017, she helped launch the 'What's Your Mission?' charitable initiative to support a children's hospital in Los Angeles.

Marley Dias

In an attempt to discover books that featured young black girls like her, Marley Dias began the #1000BlackGirlBooks initiative that gathered support and encouragement online, and donations from the likes of Ellen DeGeneres. She continues to champion diversity in books and encourage reading.

Yara Shahidi

Having been in front of the camera since she was six years old, Yara has grown up in the spotlight and continues to use her platform to promote equality and acceptance. Not only is she a talented actress, a heartfelt activist and a fashion icon, she is also heading to Harvard with a recommendation letter from the one and only Michelle Obama in her back pocket!

THE BIG QUIZ

So you've finished the book and brushed up on your influencer knowledge. Now it's time to put your new-found expertise to the test! Try out this quiz, then flick to page 95 to see how well you've done.

1

What did Maddie Ziegler's parents almost name her?

a. Amy

b. Taylor

c. Christine

2

What is Storm Reid's favourite snack?

a. Mint oreos

b. Custard creams

c. Chocolate chip cookies

3

What happened during Maddie Ziegler and Millie Bobby Brown's first sleepover?

a. They stayed up watching films and ate too many sweet treats

b. The fire alarm went off in the middle of the night

c. They saw a ghost

4

Match the celebrity with their fluffy friend.

JoJo   Maliboo

Mackenzie   Nala

Zoella   BowBow

Sophia Grace   Poppy

5

Which of our fave female celebs has a secret (or not-so-secret, if you're one of her 100 million followers!) knack for baking?

a. Taylor Swift

b. Zendaya

c. Ariana Grande

6

Which faces have been scrambled here?

A

B

C

7 What does Sophie Grace have a huge fear of?

a. Lifts

b. Spiders

c. Heights

8 How old was Storm Reid when she starred in her very first short film?

a. 3

b. 7

c. 9

9 True or false, Dove Cameron wore three different wigs in *Descendants 2*?

True   **False**

Each of the *Dance Moms* girls have a signature dance move. In which series did Nia learn her signature move?

a. Series three

b. Series six

c. Series one

Which of our favourite sibling acts first appeared on YouTube at a mere eighteen months old?

a. Maddie and Mackenzie

b. Brooklyn and Bailey

c. The Haschak Sisters

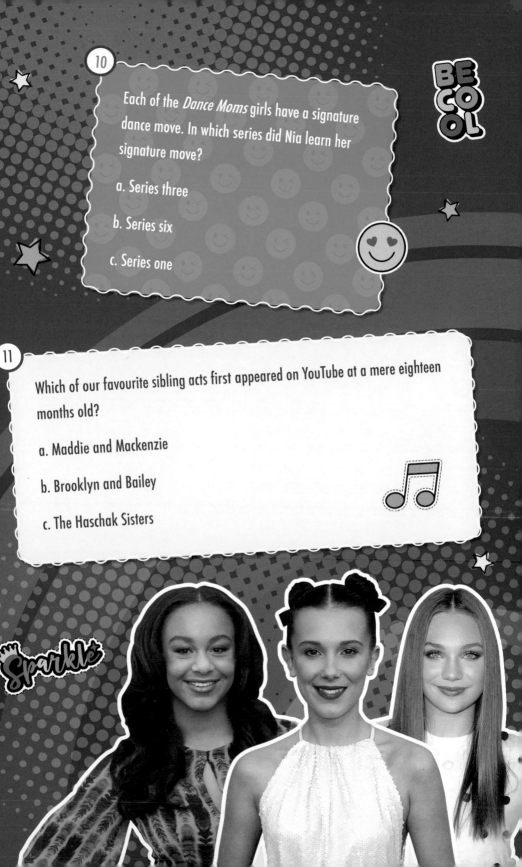

12

Which amazing woman told Storm Reid not to worry about things she couldn't change?

a. Mindy Kaling

b. Reese Witherspoon

c. Oprah Winfrey

13

Which *Dance Moms* girl has launched her own book club?

a. Nia

b. Chloe

c. Maddie

14

What's one way of telling the difference between Lisa and Lena?

a. Lena is slightly taller than Lisa

b. Lena has braces and Lisa doesn't

c. Lena wears glasses and Lisa doesn't

15

Which celebrity did Sophia Grace and Rosie not meet on *The Ellen Show*?

a. Taylor Swift

b. Justin Bieber

c. Harry Styles

SCORES ARE IN

Now that you've taken the quiz, flick to page 95 to discover how well you did. Then add up your answers to reveal your score.

0–5 Celebrity Sloppy

JoJo who? Musical.ly what? Your celeb knowledge may not be top-notch, but don't sweat it. It doesn't matter if you don't know your Maddie Z from your Millie BB – what matters is that you're having fun and following your dreams!

5–10 Celebrity Savvy

From super-cool Zendaya to inspirational Nia, you're pretty strong on your influencer knowledge. Be inspired by these amazing gals and spend time doing what you love!

10–15 Celebrity Spot On

Wow, you are TOTALLY clued up about Maddie, JoJo, Lauren and the rest of these awesome influencers! Just make sure you're not spending *toooo* much time online – the real world is fun too.

BELIEVE IN YOU

So you've reached the end of the book – and you're probably feeling pretty inspired by the passionate, talented and empowering girls you've met within these pages. Take in some last words of wisdom from these wonderful young women, then plan your own awesome goals for the future.

Taylor Swift

'If you're lucky enough to be different from everyone else, don't change!'

Chloe Lukasiak

'To anyone who has ever been told that they can't do it, that they shouldn't do it or they aren't good enough — ignore it. Do it anyways and prove them wrong.'

How are you going to take the first steps in following your dreams?

Today I will...

1. ....

2. ....

3. ....

This week I will...

1. ....

2. ....

3. ....

This year I will...

1. ....

2. ....

3. ....

ANSWERS

Page 28

B

Page 53

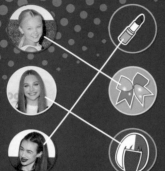

Page 62

A – 4

B – 3

C – 5

D – 1

E – 2

Page 66

Pages 82–83

Pages 86–91

1. b

2. a

3. b

4. JoJo – BowBow

Mackenzie – Maliboo

Zoella – Nala

Sophia Grace – Poppy

5. a

6.

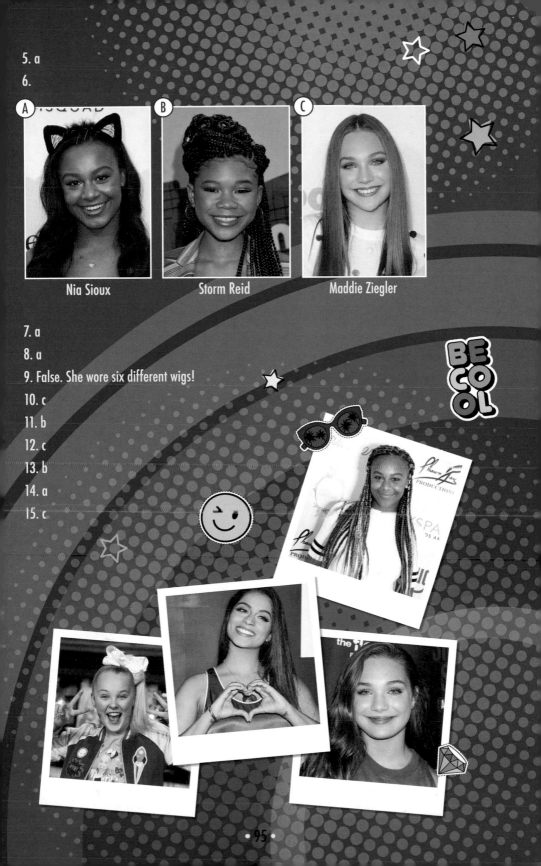

A   Nia Sioux

B   Storm Reid

C   Maddie Ziegler

7. a

8. a

9. False. She wore six different wigs!

10. c

11. b

12. c

13. b

14. a

15. c

BE CO OL